African Bullfrog as Pets

A Complete African Bullfrog Pet Owner's Guide

African Bullfrog breeding, where to buy, types, care, temperament, cost, health, handling, diet, and much more included!

By: Lolly Brown

Foreword

Bringing a pet into your life is a great idea. You will have a companion during high times and low times. However, you need to thoroughly research a certain pet before you buy one.

You may want to consider having a frog as your next home companion. You still need to research the breed as every breed requires different care, just like any other animals. If you have thoroughly researched the breed, this will allow you to understand its need, where to buy, food needed, and the habitat you need to provide.

Any animal can be a great first pet for any child or family, as long as you provide enough parental support, education, and supervision. You need to teach all the members of the household how to behave around the frog and how to properly take care of it.

African Bullfrog are not your typical dwarf cawed frogs or the White's tree frog, but they have some similarities. This breed is a large, classic looking frog which is from Africa but can be found across the world.

This frog is not the cuddly type; they are known to be bad-tempered and somehow combative. If you will not bother it, you will get along well with your pet. This book will help you get to know our beloved African Bullfrog. Enjoy!

Table of Contents

Introduction

African Bullfrogs are considered to be the largest frog found in southern Africa! Imagine some reach the size of your dinner plate!

Both male and female are dull green in color that is paired with a cream or yellow underside. Younger frogs have yellowish stripes on their back, which will eventually fade when they mature. Aside from this, this breed boasts to have a round body with a large mouth and head.

The African Bullfrog is easily satisfied as they can and will eat anything that it can overpower and fit into its mighty mouth.

Unlike your typical pets, frogs have specific things to do during specific seasons. In some seasons, they only stay in deep soil and cover itself with a cocoon. On rainy days, this breed will congregate and will breed in temporary, shallow pools of water.

During the rainy season, your frogs will be in groups to successfully breed. Males will combat and may become very aggressive for their territory and right to breed with their counterpart.

Different from their frog families, this breed is very easy to take care. They just require a simple tank, adequate water, and a simple substrate will do them good.

This breed is slow moving, and most of the time, lethargic. Another plus is that they eat eagerly and will eating that comes into their way. They have strong jaws with sharp tooth-like processors that will bite anything immediately.

Introduction

Taking care of a frog is different from a standard pet such as a dog or a cat. Frogs need substrate to live in; the aquarium needs to have several regions for your pet to be in, a feeding and breeding schedule, and when to clean the aquarium.

We will be helping you get to know your pet easily so you will move in with your beloved African bullfrog in no time.

Chapter One: Origin and Characteristics

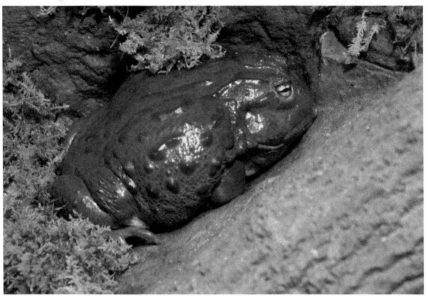

African bullfrogs are considered to be one of the biggest frogs in the whole world! They are robust and large creatures that are a great first pet for you and your family.

These breed are known to be ferocious eaters that will eat whatever you will give them. Just be careful about your fingers, or your housemates' fingers, as it may cause you to lose your beloved finger easily. In creating a conducive environment of your African bullfrog, you need to provide both land and water environment. They need to have the land environment as they bury themselves in the ground and keep themselves in a cocoon. The water environment is meant for breeding purposes. The females need the water to reproduce easily.

Picking a frog as your pet may be a different and rocky path ahead. However, picking this pet may bring you inner peace you have not found before. African bullfrogs are very slow creature and most of the time, are lethargic. So, you would not want to worry about taking it out or finding it elsewhere.

In this chapter, we will be giving you the essential information about the African bullfrog. We will be including biological facts, short history. This information will help you in learning and taking care of the species. This, together with the other chapters, will help you understand your new chosen pet, the African Bullfrog.

The Breed's Origin

Belonging to the family of Pyxicephalidae, the African Bullfrog is also known as the pixie frog. However, you should not be fooled about the name, because this will grow as big as your plate!

They are mostly found in Botswana, Malawi, Namibia, Swaziland, Zambia, Congo, Angola, Kenya, Mozambique, South Africa, Tanzania, and Zimbabwe.

The African Bullfrog tends to live in dry savanna, subtropical, moist savanna, tropical dry shrub land, intermittent freshwater marshes, intermittent freshwater lakes, arable land, pasture lands, ditches, and canals.

Do not fret as these species are the least concern in terms of extinctions, which means that they are very far from being extinct.

Size, Life Span, and Physical Appearance

African Bullfrogs are also known as the giant bullfrogs. They are the largest amphibian that lives in South Africa. This breed reaches around 2 kg in weight and 20 to 25 cm in length for males, while their female counterpart only reaches half of their size. This breed is considered as one of the few breed of frogs where the males are larger than the females.

Many people would create food items from the African bullfrogs, however, this frog contains poison that would cause kidney failures and even death, especially if you ingest or intake it in large amounts. This breed is known to live up to 20 years in captivity, but if they are left on their own, they can live up to 40.

Aside from this, the African bullfrog is very unique as they can dig holes using their legs. They love to spend their time in the water and land equally. This breed has easily adapted to their environment. A distinct feature of this breed is that they have three teeth that protrude from their lower jaw, we must stress out that these teeth are 'canine-like', which means it can possibly rip up anything! The bullfrogs use their teeth to fight off their predators as well as to hold their prey easily. Be very careful as your hand could be the next food of your beloved African Bullfrog.

Its front teeth are known to draw blood from its prey. Adult frogs are known to be very aggressive if you have provoked them, aside from it, you will see them swell up if they start intimidating you.

These frogs are large bodied with a distinct feature of broad ridged backs paired with their powerful hind legs. Most of these frogs are olive green in color, but the difference between the sexes concerns their underbellies. Male frogs have orange or yellow throat and belly, while females have creamy beige underneath.

Quick Facts

Scientific Classification: Kingdom Animalia, Phylum Chrodata, Class Amphibia, Order Anura, Pyxicephalidae family, Genus Pyxicephaulus, and known as P. adspersus

Distribution and Range: this breed is scattered in Angola, Kenya, Mozambique, South Africa, Tanzania, Zimbabwe, Botswana, Malawi, Namibia, Swaziland, Zambia, and Congo.

Breed Size: small to medium size

Body Type and Appearance: The African Bullfrog is a large-bodied breed. They boast to have a distinct feature of broad ridged backs and have powerful hind legs that could dig up holes in the dirt.

Length: male African bullfrogs can reach 23 cm or 9 inches, while females are much smaller.

Weight: Males can weigh from 1.4 kg or 3.1 lbs. to 2 kg or 4.4 lb. Females are known to be smaller than their male counterpart.

Skin Texture: slippery or slimy

Color: both sexes are olive green in color but each sex has its own distinct color of either yellow or orange.

Temperament: The African Bullfrog is a great first amphibian for beginner pet owners. It is very easy to take care of and they are a hardy specie, which means it rarely becomes ill. However, you may need to worry about its predatory tendencies. It will anything that will move, so you may need to keep your frog alone. It will become very aggressive, so you need to be careful wherever you put the finger. Your frog may mistake your finger as a food and might bite it. After the incident, do not pull away the hand from the frog's jaw as you may injure your pet, put your frog under running water and soon enough, your frog would let go.

Diet: The African bullfrog is known to be carnivorous frogs. They prey on animals of their same size or even smaller size. They can eat a variety of creatures such as worms, roaches, locusts, crickets. Do not be surprised if you see them eating small birds, amphibians, mammals, and even reptiles. In captivity, you should feed them worms, mice, roaches, or rats. If you keep multiple frogs, better have them in separate aquariums as one might eat the other, especially if they are of different sizes.

Habitat: Since they are both freshwater - dwelling, and terrestrial amphibian, these African bullfrog hibernate in drier savanna when they do not really like their environment. They will come out during rainy seasons, which is also their breeding season. They are active during the day during this season; this phenomenon is known as diurnal. You should not be surprise if you see that your pet is not moving as they can become dormant for around 10 months, which will stretch up to even two years if the season is not right for breeding.

Health Condition: This breed does not really have lot health problems. However, fungal and bacterial infections in the eyes and skins are common. Aside from this, your pet might experience internal parasites and even ammonia poisoning.

Behavior: This breed croak loudly to let the owner know that it is feeling stressed. The African Bullfrog makes great pet as long as you know what you are doing. Do not provoke or mess with them and they won't cuddle you. However, you will have an easy to take care of amphibian that will last a long time.

Life Span: twenty years if kept in captivity and forty if kept in the wild.

These are the essential information that you need to know about the African bullfrog. These are essential because your chosen pet will last you for longer than 20 years! Having a frog in your life is long-term commitment so you need to be ready to give it the best environment it can have.

You still need to know a lot of things to take care of your pet frog. You need to know the substrate, feeding guidelines, breeding, and other things to do to make the frog's life easy. These frogs are a breeze to take care of if you know what to do with them, especially when problem arises.

However, these little creatures are a breeze to take care; you would not even feel that you have a pet when you have managed to provide its initial needs. If you still want to own an African bullfrog, read on to know more! Enjoy reading.

Chapter Two: Treating the African Bullfrog as Family

We have now discussed the basic characteristics and background information about the African Bullfrog. We also have given you a 'cheat' sheet of the important information about this frog. You now need to know if getting a frog is truly right for you. In this section, we will be dwelling more about this frog; its behavioral traits, estimated budget, and permits and licenses that you will need to have. There are things that you need to buy before welcoming the first African Bullfrog at home. You might think that they are easy to take care of, but buying an African Bullfrog is a holistic commitment. Let us start this chapter and further know our beloved pet, African Bullfrog.

What Makes It a Great Pet?

Buying a pet is a great idea, whether you live alone or with your family. However, you need to think through and through before you purchase your first pet because it is a big and difficult decision.

When you have chosen your pet, you need to put all of your heart and soul to take care of this creature as if your own child. If you want to try something new, buying an African Bullfrog is great choice for you.

You might be scared of buying amphibians because they require different things as your typical mammal pets. African Bullfrog are easily available almost everywhere. They are dormant creatures that won't need too much food because they rarely move. However, they have aggressive tendencies. You need to be very careful about taking care of this pet.

Temperament and Behavioral Characteristics

- They have sensitive skin.

- They can live up to 40 years if you meet all of its needs.

- Male African Bullfrogs will guard their tadpoles, but sometimes may eat them if they are stressed out or in the wild.

- You can't cuddle these little creatures.

- They have sharp teeth and could bite humans when handled or provoked.

- They have low exercise routines.

- They like to stay in a pond with only is head floating.

- They hate to have other frogs interfere in their

territory.

We have just rounded up the behavioral characteristics as well as its temperament of the African Bullfrog. You could also know new traits and characteristics as you raise this frog on your own.

Why Choose African Bullfrog?

In this portion, we will be giving you pros and cons on why you should purchase your very first African Bullfrog as your next household pet. You need to go through each bullet because this will help you in making your decision.

Pros

- African bullfrog can make great display pets.
- Relatively low maintenance.
- After all the initial costs, caring for frogs is very inexpensive.

Cons

- You should only purchase your pet African Bullfrog from legitimate pet traders.

- The habitat can be difficult to keep healthy and clean.

- Some frogs are sensitive to waste and other contaminants.

- They are not really great for kids.

- It can be difficult to find someone to take care of your frog when you are away.

- You need to handle insects if you want to feed your African Bullfrog.

If you still plan to own an African Bullfrog after going through its pros and cons, you need to continue to know more about the breed. You need to know the costs and licenses that you need to acquire before you purchase it.

Licenses for Your African Bullfrog

If you have decided to legally purchase your African Bullfrog, you need to have the frog licensed so you and your frog can be protected, and you will follow the rules and regulation of the state you are currently living.

Here are some guidelines that you need to know to license your African Bullfrog:

- Some states will require you to obtain a license before you own your frog.
- You need to check the laws, as well as the rules and regulation before you decide that you want to legally own your frog in your area.
- If you want to move to a different state, you need to know the specific license requirements of the state that you want to move in.
- You should only purchase your frog from a registered and reputable frog breeder.

Can You Handle the Costs?

If you want to own an African Bullfrog, you need to prepare many things. You need to find the best breeder and best place to buy the African bullfrog; you also need to purchase an enclosure or aquarium or tank, food bowls and water dishes, and different supplies such as different bulbs for heat sources, food supplies and supplements, and other essentials.

If you know you have a budget for this task, let us go out and buy our African Bullfrog!

Costs of Keeping an African Bullfrog

Having a new companion in your life is never easy at first. You need to plan and prepare everything before this companion comes into your life. Getting a new pet in your life is like having a child; you need to provide the pet with food, shelter, water, and other basic necessities. In this case, you need to allot money for this task.

Keeping a great budget might be difficult, but you will soon get a hang of it if you start to early and plan it well. The total budget for your African Bullfrog will heavily depend on the type and kind of sources that you will purchase. Some items might be more expensive because of limited stocks. Aside from this, you need to keep in mind the quality of the product and how long it will last for your frog. Sometimes, cheaper does not really mean 'cheap' - because it will not last a long time. In this portion, we will give you a breakdown of the budget needed for your pet, African Bullfrog

African Bullfrog's Price

Prices for the African Bullfrog's vary greatly in price. You need to remember that you need to buy the bullfrog from reputable frog breeder. The price of the African Bullfrog varies from $40 to $400, depending on the age and gender.

A newly-born frog can be as low as $40, however, if the frog is already big, or the same size as you plate, the price can go as high as $500. You need to be prepared to shell out this kind of money. Find a breeder of store where you can buy a well-taken care of frog.

Other Essentials

Aside from buying the frog, you need to be financially prepared of all other essentials that you need to purchase. These things are important to keep your pet alive and healthy. Some of these things are only a one time purchase, while some are recurrent expenses. Find the best option in the market so you can be sure that you will keep your frog very satisfied and to get the best value for your money.

Housing Requirements

- You need to buy a captive breed of the African Bullfrog. We will get into detail on why captives are better than wild frogs.

- As a rule, you need to only keep one frog per housing space. Bullfrogs can't be together because they might kill or eat one another.

- An adult African Bullfrog can fit into a 36" x 18" x 18" enclosure. Make sure you buy a large enclosure for your pet to jump around and hide on.
- The price of the enclosure starts at $20 but can shoot up to $50. This well depends on the brand and the material used.

- Some enclosures are built with different apparatus to handle your pet very well.

- As you want to buy a frog, you need to purchase a bedding in which your pet can burrow into.

- Beddings start at $5 but can be as high as $10.

- Make sure you have enough bedding to keep your pet very satisfied.

Temperature and Lighting

- African Bullfrogs need temperature gradient to control their body temperature.

- You need to provide a cool and hot side of the chosen enclosure.

- All the hot parts should be kept together as well as the cold parts. In this way, your frog can choose which side it will stay on.

- The warmer side should be between 78 and 85, while the other parts should be in normal temperature.

- You need to buy good temperature gauges to know

the exact temperature of the enclosure.

- The price of the gauge can be around $5 to $40, but this depends on the kind. The $5 is a dial thermometer while the $40 is digital.

- At night, the temperature may drop, you need to purchase heat pads to keep your pet warm and cozy. The heat pads costs around $50 - $100. The difference depends on the watts it will give.

- In the wild, African Bullfrogs do not really receive too much heat, specifically the UVB rays. You do not need to buy UVB lights but supplement it with food enriched with Vitamin D3.

Humidity

- You need to provide an enough size of water bowl paired with fresh water.

- Always change the water daily.

- Just like any other amphibians, these little guys are very sensitive to toxins around their environment.

- Do not use any harsh products, candles, or incense in the room where you will place your frog.

- Do not, also, smoke in the room where your frog is staying. Frogs absorb the chemicals in their skin, so you might unknowingly kill your pet.

- Start with the humidity at 60%. You need to mist the enclosure once or twice a day to provide enough moisture for your pet.
- You can also buy a humidity gauge to set-up the correct range for your pet.

- A hand mister values at $3 apiece, however, you might need to set an alarm every time you need to mist your beloved pet's aquarium.

- However, you can also buy monsoon sprayer, but this can be as high as $300. But this apparatus is already automatic.

- You should not give distilled water to your African Bullfrog, either at its water dish or pond, as they lack minerals that your bullfrog needs for survival.

Food Requirements

- African bullfrogs are very hungry eaters.
- You need to give a diversified diet for your bullfrog.
- They can eat crickets, phoenix worms, horned worms, wax worms, earthworms, mealworms, silk worms, and even roaches.
- You can feed your bullfrog using tweezers.
- Aside from this, you can also give canned feeder insects.
- You need to supplement the frog's diet through dusting their food with calcium.

These are just the initial things that you need to prepare if you want to raise your African Bullfrog on your own. Make sure you have these items ready before you bring your frog at home. If you do not prepare the things beforehand,

Chapter Two: The Treating the African Bullfrog as Family

you might have a difficult time taking care of your frog and setting up a place for it to live in.

Chapter Three: Housing Needs for Your African Bullfrog

At this point, you have now fully decided that you want to acquire the majestic African Bullfrog. You now have enough essential information about the pet of your choosing. Aside from this, you now know what things to prepare to welcome your pet at home.

You need to communicate well with your friends, family, and other breeders for further information. However, the task of welcoming your African Bullfrog at home is not yet done.

After buying the African Bullfrog, you must now prepare a sustainable habitat, caging, and needs of your pet. You need to prepare this before you even think of handling, breeding, or even taking them at home.

A sustainable and conducive environment is a big part of making your pet's life healthy and happy. This would also help your pet not become too stressed out.

There are things that you need to prepare and buy before you buy your African Bullfrog at home. If you do not provide these things, you will have a hard time balancing taking care of your pet and buying the necessary things.

You can easily buy supplies from big pet stores, and some, even big supermarkets. Buy the supplies first before you go home. In this portion, we will help you give the best house for your pet African Bullfrog. Take note of these requirements because this will be a breeze.

Housing Requirements

Frogs are reptiles. They need both water and land to survive their life. Aside from this, frogs need certain humidity in order to maintain its skin texture. They also need light, but not too much light, just enough not to dry out their skin. Providing these things will make sure that your frog will have a happy life when it is with you.

Here is the overview of the things you need to provide for your African Bullfrog:

- Substrate, such as moss, fibers, sands
- Water dish
- Food bowl (which is just optional, you can use the water dish as the food bowl)
- logs
- plants
- lamps
- thermometer
- terrarium humidifier or mister
- tank
- water
- hidey-huts
- water filter
- hygrometer

- submersible aquarium heater and under-tank heating pad
- water pump
- fake water pall
- Critter carrier, which are used for vet visits, quarantines, and a place to put your frogs when you are cleaning the main tank.

This portion will give you a detailed data about the things you need to prepare for your African Bullfrog's first day in your life.

Aquarium

Before you even buy your African Bullfrog, you need to make sure that you have already set-up the house a week in advance. This move will ensure that you to check all the components of the frog house you are working on. There are many kinds of aquarium that you can purchase, but more on that later.

The size of the cage should be around 40 gallon, or 170L. This would provide enough room for your frog to maneuver around the terrarium. These are the kinds of aquarium that you can buy:

- Terrestrial Tank

    This tank is suited for frogs who prefer drier climate. This will just consist of a substrate and a water supply that could either be a water bowl or a small pool. House frogs do not really like this environment in the long run.

- Aquatic Tank

    This tank is just the same set-up as for fish, or in short, an aquarium with water.

- Half and Half Tank

    This is the most common set-up that you can do. This will consist of half water and half land aquarium set-up. You can do this in a lot of ways, you can fill the tank with water and then put in large rocks to become land-masses. You can also buy special separators to divide water and land masses.

- Arboreal Tank

This tank is for frogs who like to stay up high on tree branches. Essentially, you will purchase a tall tank and put small trees beside it.

Lighting Equipment

You need to figure out the correct lighting and temperature requirement for your African Bullfrog. Make sure you do a thorough research before you set-up your tank.

Unlike other pets, such as snakes, lizards, and turtles, frogs do not totally need special lighting, such as UVB. Frogs can get their vitamin D requirements through food and supplements.

You still need to provide light source that would last up to 12 hours a day, especially if the African Bullfrog's tank does not have enough access to natural light. You may opt to buy fluorescent lighting for the aquarium; these kinds of bulbs do not get too hot. Lights that emit too much light is very dangerous to your frogs, your frog might jump up and it could hurt them so much.

Ventilation

Humidity and ventilation are two key factors in keeping your frogs a success. You need to constantly spray your frog's tank to maintain the correct humidity; you can also buy an automatic mister so you will not be bothered to spray it throughout the day.

If you are keeping live plants with your pet, you also need to spray the plants some water so it will retain the water and moisture for a long time, this will also help to keep the level of humidity of the aquarium.

You also need to have adequate ventilation for your pet African Bullfrog. You can keep the ventilation mesh at the back or top of the cage. Without ventilation inside your tank, your cage will develop a fungus and your beloved pet might get sick and develop illnesses.

Humidifier

Frogs need humidifier especially during dry season such as summer. Mist it daily so you can keep the tank fresh.

Heat pads

Heat pads are an alternative if you want to produce heat in your African Bullfrog's cage. It will produce enough warmth for your pet. Make sure you stick it at the farthest end of the enclosure and just leave it there.

However, you need to constantly check the temperature inside the terrarium. Sometimes, heat pads could raise the temperature and it will be too hot for your African Bullfrog. Buying a heat pat could lessen the cost of buying too much light inside your tank.

Substrate

Substrates are things that you put on the bottom of the terrarium. The basic function of the substrate or the bedding is to absorb the waste your African Bullfrog created. However, there are also other purposes of the substrate, such as:

- maintain the level of humidity inside the terrarium

- it could also retain moisture inside

- it would offer a cushion against a glass bottom or a hard plastic

- it would provide a shelter for burrowing

- It could be a great source of heat for your pet.

What Substrate Do I Need To Use?

Different reptiles or amphibians need different kind of substrate. You also need to consider your African Bullfrog's feeding needs. Substrate components could be ingested and could cause blockages and impaction, so make sure to use the right kind of substrate.

In some occasions, you can mix and match different kinds of substrate. You need to also plan on how to clean your pet's cage. Here are the different kinds of substrates that you can use:

- Nothing

  In some cases, you do not really need any substrate in your frog's aquarium. You can put a drain at the bottom so you can easily hose down the aquarium. However, you may need to frequently clean the substrate as it may become unaesthetic ally pleasing.

- Newspapers and Paper towels

   You can use a layer of newspaper and/or paper towels if you are okay with the regular clean-up. However, some may need to be changed more than once a day in some situation.

   Some reptiles need paper towels as their substrate. For amphibians, you need to use plain paper towels because those with colors could be harmful. Aside from this, you need to closely pay attention on the wetness or dryness of the paper towels. Wet paper towels are breeding grounds for unwanted bacteria. Other than that, reptiles and amphibians can't really burrow under paper towels.

- Mats, Carpeting, and Liners

  This is another simple substrate option that you use for your amphibian or reptile. These things are just like your paper towels and magazines; however, you do not need to throw this out immediately. However, you may need to purchase two sets of mats, when one will be soiled, you can replace one while you wash the other one and dry it out.

  This requires frequent cleaning and not suitable for pets that needs moisture in their terrarium.

- Carefresh and other similar small animal bedding

  This kind of substrate is usually used by hamsters, guinea pigs, and other small pets. This is made of bedding and shavings made from recycled paper products. However, this is not really appropriate for amphibians because it spoils when it becomes wet.

- Moss

  You can easily find moss at garden centers and pet stores. Some of these things are ornamental, which means it should not be used as a substrate, but decors or accents in the terrarium.

  There are other mosses that are suitable to be substrates for reptiles, but not suitable for amphibians. These are the typical green mosses that you can see in pet stores that are put in bales or bricks. This kind of moss does not really hold moisture.

  The sphagnum moss can be tan, pink, or brown in color. This grows in bogs and will decay in soil additive. This kind of moss can be used alone for many amphibians and lizards. You need to place this correctly under shelters and substrates. This kind of moss is actually acidic, so it is not a good option for burrowing and terrestrial amphibians.

- Soil Blends

    There are soil mixtures easily available at your nearby pet stores. There are available soil substrates that you can use to make your own ingredients. Different soils have different characteristics. It is quite difficult to evaluate their suitability as a substrate.

    Do not use soils that have rocks, vermiculite, or perlite. You should only use soil blends that are sold from pet suppliers from direct pet suppliers.

    Soil actually works well for burrowing and terrestrial species that comes from tropical or humid environment. You still need to pay attention to the moisture content of the soil. You still need to have a drainage layer of gravel or other material so the soil does not become waterlogged.

    If the soil becomes too wet it will spoil and some types could possibly irritate the skin.

Some amphibians could possibly ingest this soil.

- Coconut Husk Fiber

  Some of these things are sold in dry compressed brick. This is made from ground up fibers of coconut. When you place this in water, this expands and becomes excellent substrates for both amphibians and reptiles. If you are able to maintain its cleanliness, you do not replace this often. This kind of substrate holds moisture well. You can mix this with other kinds of substrate blend to make your own substrate for your pet.

  However, this could cause irritation for amphibians if it has not expanded and settled down well before use. It would even spoil if it comes in contact with water for long periods of time.

- Coconut Husk Chunks

  These chunks are also available for dry compact brick. This consists of hairy coconut fibers around the coconut shell that did not fall on the ground yet. These things have similarities with coconut husk fiber, but these are larger and may be prone to be a problem if ingested by your pet. Often, this substrate is mixed with the fiber or sol. When mixed with other stuff, it really improves the drainage in a tropical terrarium.

- Leaf Litter

  This is actually collected rather than purchased in places. Leaf litter can form a bulk of your substrate that is suited for some reptiles and amphibians. This works well if mixed with soil, coconut fiber, and some other natural substrate. Magnolia and live oak are the common barks used.

  You can either used this alone; however there is a potential risk of infectious diseases or pests especially with freshly collected leaves. To prevent this, you need to wash the leaves under hot water and then have it air dry in the sun for several days. You can also microwave the leaves to kill pests.

- Fir Bark

  Previously, this is the only natural substrate for amphibians and reptiles. This fir bark is natural and can potentially retain humidity in an enclosure. However, this is not appropriate for all species. The main issue for this type of substrate is that your pet could ingest while eating.

- Cypress Mulch

  This is another substrate for amphibians and reptiles that are made from wood. This is widely available at garden centers and pet stores. This Cypress Mulch can work very well in humid or moist conditions than other substrate. You can use this for both amphibians and reptiles.

Unfortunately, this kind of substrate is not really sourced in a sustainable manner. The logging of these things damages both the wetlands and important habitat.

- Sand (play sand, calcium sand, and etc.)

  This kind of substrate can be used alone for some reptiles. Some owners use this alone, but you need to check it for rocks or debris that will cause problems when your pet ingests this. There are sands that are made from calcium carbonate, which are much safer to use because it will be less likely to have an issue with impaction.

- Gravel, Rocks, and Stones

  Many kinds of rocks, gravel, and stones are available for your pets. However, you need to be careful when using this kind of rocks as substrate. If your pet has ingested this, it will be very difficult to pass through the body.

In order to avoid the blockages, you need to use stones that are too large for your pet to swallow. Aside from this, you also need to avoid aquarium gravel; you can use this if you put it under another substrate as a drainage layer.

Chapter Four: Feeding Your African Bullfrog

Giving good nutrition is a big factor to have a healthy and happy pet. You thoroughly need to know your pet before you purchase it. Make sure you exhaustively research about the breed to know its need and wants. And an essential need of your pet is its food and nutrition.

If you do not give the correct food and nutrition to your African Bullfrog, this will compromise its health and may even end up in death. Make sure you go through each section because they are both essential and important to the life of your pet.

Frogs are carnivorous and predators, you need to give a fresh prey for your beloved African Bullfrog. However, it is more than just dumping preys into the terrarium. Just like any other pet, the diet depends well on the species, age, and breeding status.

This portion will give you nutritional guideline for your African Bullfrog. We have also included some feeding tips, frequency, and amounts and what to give and what not to give to your pet.

What Does My African Bullfrog Eat?

Adult frogs need a regular diet of insects; some breeds might even need small vertebrates, such as mice, and or fish to stay healthy. These fresh preys should be alive when you give it to them.

In the wild, these frogs are opportunistic feeders; they will truly eat whatever you put it. You may want to copy this experience when you will be keeping your African Bullfrogs at home. Proper nutrition and feeding is more than just dropping random insects and preys inside the terrarium.

Gut - load diet is the process of increasing the nutritional value of the prey that you are going to feed your pet 48 hours before you serve it to them. We all live in an ecosystem and we all benefit from each other one way or another. A good example is the food chain. In which an animal preys on another animal and eventually the predator becomes the prey of another animal as well. The nutrients contained by the prey will pass on to its predator and so on.

In captivity, it is impossible for you to create the same natural cycle present in the wild but gut loading can be an alternative in order to replicate this process.

By this way, if you feed high nutritional value food to the prey you are about to serve, your pet will also receive the nutrients you have loaded to its meal. Make sure that the right kind of vitamins or nutrients will be passed in order to achieve balanced nutrition

Usually, in order to successfully gut load the prey you are providing, there is a need for you to administer multivitamin powder with calcium. Be mindful that phosphorus inhibits calcium absorption therefore the level of calcium should be higher than the phosphorus level. Its oxalates content should also be at minimum.

Most commercial gut loads you can purchase are low in calcium which may not be enough for the nutritional needs of your frog. Do not worry since you can formulate your own gut loading recipe. By this way you can save money and really make sure that the nutritional content will be exceptional. Below are the steps you can make use of in choosing the right ingredients for your gut load formula:

- Choose what kind of food you are going to use for gut loading your frog's food. You may choose between fruits and vegetables. Have at least 2 or 3 options. Serve it alternately every now and then.

- Make sure that the fruits and vegetables of your choice are free from any chemical residue like pesticides. Rinse it thoroughly under fresh running water. These chemical components can be toxic to so make sure the foods are properly rinsed.

- The nutrient content of the prey you have gut loaded will pass on your frog after 2 to 3 weeks of consuming.

How Much and How Often Do I Need To Feed My African Bullfrog?

Unlike other pets, frogs have a high risk of obesity due to overeating. Since they are opportunistic feeder, they will eat until they are out of food, this scenario could cause them to be ill. You need to offer mice or other calorie-enriched food just in moderation. The rule of the thumb, feed the young adult five to seven crickets or any other insects several times per week.

Some Food Suggestions
Crickets

Crickets are easily available at any pet stores at a cheap price. These are great food for your African Bullfrog because they can be alive for a long time while inside the aquarium.

You need to feed the cricket potatoes so it can gain

necessary vitamins, but also get water from the slices. These little creatures provide great nutrition and very easy to acquire.

Meal Worms

These meal worms can be quickly raised by putting the adult beetles that is put inside a container or fish tank. You need to fill the bottom of the said container with oats, carrots, or even potatoes to allow the worms and adults to acquire water.

These things grow quickly and can provide you with about 500 meal worm per breeding cycle!

Night crawlers and Red Worms

You can easily buy these things at any fishing bait shop. A great fact is that your frog will surely love them. These worms are a major food source for your frogs. Red worms are active little creatures that and your frog will surely love to chase them.

You can also go into your yard and collect nightcrawlers by turning over several logs and rocks. They naturally occur in moist areas of the yard and even the forest. You can also collect frogs by raking up leaves that pile up in your yard.

Roaches

This is actually uncommon for frog diets because they are not easily available. However, they are high in vitamins, proteins, and other nutrients.

There are different species of roaches that you can feed to your frog. Dubia and discoid roaches are not suitable for small frogs as the can become too large. Nymph and juvenile roaches have softer bodies and smaller, so it can be easily eaten and digested by your African Bullfrog. Latteralis roaches are smaller but they are fast. This kind of roach may be difficult for slower frogs to catch.

Canned Insects and Traps

There are brands that would help you to collect moths and other insects. Canned insects, such as snails, grasshoppers, and silkworms can be easily fed to your African Bullfrog.

Fish and Mice

Feeding pink or adult mice would cause your pet to have problems in the eyes, kidney, and liver. You can give it but in moderate amount.

You can feed mice to your African Bullfrog only once for 7 to 10 days only. If you feed more than enough, your pet might suffer from liver problems and fur impaction.

Commercially - Grown Invertebrates

During months you can't collect wild-caught insects, such as winter. The diet of your African Bullfrog should not only be crickets, however, it should be a great mix of earthworm, crickets, roaches, and waxworms.

There are many dealers of silkworms and tomato hornworms. You can also add supplements such as calcium and vitamin D3 to the preys.

Frequently Asked Questions
Do I Need To Give Supplements and Vitamins?

Your frog needs vitamin A and D because these things can't be produced by your African Bullfrog. You need to include "gut loaded" insects; these are insects that you have fed with vitamin-rich food.

What Prey Size Should I Give My African Bullfrog?

You only need to give preys that are smaller than the width of the frog's head, or else, your African Bullfrog's intestine could be impacted.

What Should I Not Give to My African Bullfrog?

You should not give fruits and vegetables to your African Bullfrog because they are strictly meat eater. Aside from this, you should not give human table scraps, commercial food that are meant for other pets, preys that are too large for them, or even wild-caught insects, as this could pose a great risk of pesticide or even a parasite infection.

Other insects like ladybugs, millipedes, stinkbugs, and praying mantis are toxic for your African Bullfrog to digest. Also add to this list are "hairy" caterpillars, spiders, and other invertebrate that could possibly sting or bite. Do not also collect brightly colored insect, such as fireflies because they are toxic.

What Do They Drink?

Giving your pet happy nutrition is incomplete without de-chlorinated water. You can give them tap water as long as you treat it to remove chlorine. There are many de-chlorinators available at supply stores and even online.

Before giving tap water, make sure you check it for harmful elements that could make your frog very sick. Do not be shocked if your frog do not drink or sip from a bottle. Frog absorbs water through their bodies.

A way for the frog to get water is through spraying the tank to have enough hydration and as well as keeping the humidity high.

These are the important things that you need to give to your African Bullfrog. These are just some primers that will make your pet happy and healthy as well as alive for a long time. There are some other necessities that you would come across in the future; however, you may need to experience it in order to know it. Plan each meal properly and make sure you stock up on prey, especially during colder months. You do not want to starve your pet by not feeding them enough or not giving enough nutrients.

Chapter Five: Breeding Your African Bullfrog

There comes a period where your frog needs or even wants to breed. Breeding your frog could extend its generation for a couple of years. However, they are a lot of considerations that you need to do if you want to breed your pet. You need to know the proper timing, season, and frog to mate with. You need to remember that you do not breed your pet just to sake for the money; you need to breed it for the continuing of its breed and generation. Aside from this, you need to know the life cycle of the frog before you truly start breeding it.

The Life Cycle of Your African Bullfrog

When the breeding starts, which we will discuss at a later part of this book, the male frog is usually clasp to its mate. This starts the fertilization of the egg.

Spawn

When the male is attached to its female, the male fertilizes the female eggs as these eggs are laid. It is a common knowledge that frogs lay eggs in hundreds, however toads lay eggs in long chains.

It is a usual behavior that frogs leave at this point, but some frogs stick around to watch their eggs. Some frogs develop unusual ways of caring for their babies.

Eggs

Both toads and frogs lay many eggs; however, there are many hazards between the fertilization and its maturity.

These eggs may die when it turns white or opaque. The lucky eggs manage to hatch and start a journey that is full of perils.

The frog's life starts when the central yolk is split into two. After this division, this further divides into four, then eight, until it looks like a raspberry on a jello cup.

After this, the embryo soon enough looks like a tadpole; it will become longer and moving in its egg.

Around 6 to 21 days after the frog fertilization, the egg will hatch. These eggs could be found in static or calm water, this is to stop getting too much rumbled in infancy. Some frog even mate in tree branches.

Tadpoles

After hatching, the tadpole still feeds in the remaining yolk, which is still in its gut. The tadpole now consists of poorly developed gills, a tail, and a mouth. At this point, the tadpole is still fragile. The tadpoles usually stick themselves to floating grasses or weeds in the water, they use their sticky little organs that are found between their belly and mouth area.

After seven to 10 days after the tadpoles had hatched, it will swim around and feed on algae.

After a month, the gills will begin to grow over the skin, until it disappears. The tadpoles have teeny tiny teeth which will help them chew their food to turn it to soupy oxygenated particles. These tadpoles have long coiled guts that would help them digest nutrients from their meadger diet. These tadpoles now become social creatures! Some interact like fishes!

Tadpoles, but with legs!

After six to nine weeks, tadpoles develop little tiny legs. Their heads will become more distinct and their body will elongate. The diet may grow to include other items such as plants and dead insects. The tadpole's arms will begin to bulge, then pop out, beginning with its elbow.

After nine weeks, the tadpole now becomes a teeny frog with a very long tail. It is on its way to be fully grown.

A Froglet or a Young Frog

At 12 weeks, these tadpoles with legs will begin to look like a miniature adult frog. Eventually, these will leave the water, but could return to the water to lay more eggs. Thus, repeating its life cycle.

Frog

By 12 to 16 weeks, but still well depends on the food and water supply, your frog should have completed its whole life cycle. These frogs will start the whole process again; they will find new mates and create a new family.

Frog Reproduction

You have probably learned about frog reproduction in your school. Well, the basics are they lay in water, it will hatch eggs then tadpoles will become into frogs. However, half of these frogs follow these specific steps, but all of the frogs only reproduce sexually and they will all hatch eggs.

In all cases of the frog, the egg fertilization will happen outside of the female bodies instead of the inside.

The female will release the eggs and the male will release the sperm at the same time.

To fully mate, they will get into a mating posture called the *amplexus,* to fully make sure that the sperm reaches the eggs. The male climbs on the female and claps all of his forelegs around the middle. Both frogs would even stay in this position for hours or even days, as the female could possibly release a hundred or more eggs.

In most cases, you can easily tell male frogs from the female frogs. We call these things such as sexual dimorphic, which mean there are a lot differences between the colors and bodies of the male and females. Other than this, male frogs would often produce a release call or a mating call when they are clasped by another male.

All of the eggs need moisture in order to develop and then most frogs will abandon their eggs once they are fertilized. However, not all eggs incubate underwater or without enough parental care. Few breeds would carry their eggs in their abdomen and vocal cords. Some would lay their eggs in dry area, then, they would keep watch of these eggs and moisten it through urine or water. Depending on the species and climate, the eggs could hatch in between a few days to a few weeks.

In some species, froglets would hatch out from the eggs, but most of the time, frogs start their lives as a tadpole. Tadpoles could become omnivores or vegetarians, but frogs are fully carnivorous beings. Some tadpoles would only eat algae, while some who have teeth could eat anything from rotting vegetation to other tadpoles. Tadpoles are voracious eaters; it would take a lot of their energy to fully complete their metamorphosis into frogs.

Tadpoles like to live in temporary rainwater pond then would become frogs in a couple of weeks.

Breeding your Frogs

Breeding your frogs can be an exciting event in your life. You can watch these translucent eggs develop into tadpoles. You need to be ready for the intense work you will do if you would want to raise your own frog colony.

Ask yourself these things:

- Am I dedicated and knowledgeable to be a frog breeder?
- Do I have time to fully take care of these tadpoles and raise them properly?
- Am I experienced enough to keep alive specie for more than a year?
- Do I have homes and destinations lined up for when these frogs grow up?

You will spend a lot of money than you might think. As we have said earlier, monetary gain should never be your first goal in this endeavor. In most cases, first time breeders may barely break even. You will need to purchase or provide several things such as rain - chambers, nursery tanks, filters, water conditioners, lighting, filters, heating, tiny insects, morph tanks, and other necessary things. You need to spend an extensive amount of cash from the beginning.

The goal of breeding should only be the love of the breed and the love for knowledge and the excitement of this specific endeavor. Some breeders may only do it with the sole intention of saving the specific species.

The ecosystem that you will provide needs to mimic their natural environment. This would give them the advantage to grow up and bring it closer to being a full grown frog. Other things that it must mimic are the rain, stress, vitamin and food sources, humidity, and warmth. You need to control the ecosystem cycling, or controlling these external factors.

Misting System

A misting routine is a system that is very critical for breeding your frog. It could be very complicated to set up on timers, but very simple if you just spray on tanks. In some cases, you need to supply the tank with heavy rains in a Rain - chamber (or a breeding chamber), if you are very serious about breeding your frogs, you would develop this chamber.

The Rain - chamber

If you plan to be an avid frog breeder, you need to have rain - chamber. This is a necessary tool that would help start the breeding cycle in the colony.

Preparing the Tank

If you already have an aquarium for your frog, you need to use a separate tank for your rain - chamber. The main purpose of this chamber is to stimulate seasonal or monsoonal rains of the frog's homeland, and this will indulge them to reproduce. The large amount of water in this chamber will create this effect.

If you only use your typical aquarium, your set-up would be destroyed by floods and dislodging plants, this might also cause fungal infections in your frogs. Even though your frogs are naturally aquatic, setting up a rain - chamber is a great idea. You would take out the egg masses out of the main tank and make them into adults, it would be easier for you to remove and fully take care of them.

The Frog Colony

In order to prepare for this event, you need to spray mist the aquariums and increase its amounts daily. However, do not over mist to the point that you can smell rotting plant materials, where your plants and soils are soaked so much that it will die.

This misting activity will start the male to croak. This would develop their nuptial pads in front of the hands. Males may even become too territorial.

Putting on Jungle Sounds

When you are ready to introduce the frogs into the tank, you may need to have a boom box placed near it, playing rain forest sounds or even their species' croaking sounds and other environmental background music.

This will help the frogs go into breeding mood. You can also look for tranquility music; however, make sure that there is no symphony music behind the rain forest sound. Make sure that you loop the sound that you will be using.

Frog Introduction

The best time to introduce the frog into their rainchamber is when the males are already calling nightly and they already have their nuptial pads ready, and the females are already ripe with their eggs. You can let the frogs stay for around a week, but not over two weeks.

Make sure that both of the frogs are fed well before the breeding process, you can also add calcium supplement to the prey that they will be eating.

Add enough water into the chamber and allow it to "rain" for around three to six hours a day. Continue this process until the frogs have already laid enough eggs. If your female frog has already laid more than enough, overbreeding may occur. Overbreeding is very unhealthy for our beloved female frog, this would deplete them with nutrients, proteins, and enzymes in their bodies which they need to continue to grow. Your females may continue to lay eggs without the hay, but it would not be fertile. Do not allow the male and female to fertilize the egg more than you can take care of.

If you can see that they have done the task, remove them immediately and sterilize again.

How to Care for Your Tadpoles

There are certain rules and regulations if you want to raise your tadpoles and keep them as frogs. You need to make sure you have researched thoroughly about this information before even breeding your frog.

Housing Tadpoles

If you plan to have your own tadpoles, make sure you have a good sized container for your tadpole, such as a swimming pool, aquarium, garden pond, or even a plastic container. You need to keep them outside that would mimic their natural environment and give them enough sunlight; however, you need to keep the container partially shaded.

Tadpoles like to have shallow water. You can place smooth gravel or rocks at the bottom of the pool. When you see that they are already maturing, they would want to get out of the water, you can place a partially submerged rock, piece of wood, or gravel that would lead to the land.

The Frogspawn

You need to have a place where you can put your frogspawn. You need to put weeds if you do not have stones or rocks. Putting weeds would do the following:

1. oxygenate the water which would help the tadpole to grow

2. The weed would have algae and bacteria on them; this will serve as your pet's main food source until they can hunt on their own.

The Water for the Tadpole Pond

If you ever plan to create a tadpole pond, you only need to give de - chlorinated fresh water. You can remove chlorine for the tap water by letting it sit for around 24 hours before you put it to the pool, or, you can treat the water with de - chlorination drops that are meant for aquariums. Tadpoles are very sensitive to chlorine and heavy metal.

In small spaces, the water needs to be frequently changed to maintain great quality. Scoop around a third of the water and replace with clean and de - chlorinated water. However, you need to remember that these tadpoles should not be handled during the water change because their skins are very sensitive to the natural oils, soaps, and chemicals that are found in our hands. Rinse your hand before and after tank maintenance, feeding, or any other task relating to your pet.

What to Feed My Tadpoles

Your tadpoles diet depend on the species, but most of the tadpoles are herbivores. You can give them thawed or frozen leafy lettuce such as spinach or romaine. You can also boil them, but boiling means a loss of nutrients, and when frozen, it is very soft enough to be eaten.

You can also give a good quality of flake fish food and crush algae tablets, which you can find at aquarium shops, at extreme cases, you can even find tadpole food at pond shops. Only feed small amounts a couple of times a day. If you feed them excessively, it will create water-quality problems. Use a small fish net to scoop out any uneaten food.

These are just some important guidelines that you need to know about breeding and the general life cycle of your frog. If you are really serious in breeding them, make sure you have enough time and money to do this task, remember, you should not do this for the money.

Aside from this, you need to have access to regular information and even a healthy support group that would help you during this endeavor. You need to have someone by your side to help you with the tasks.

Chapter Six: Setting Up Your Frog's Terrarium

In some cases, you might need to put your African Bullfrog in a temporary place. If you need to clean your aquarium and you do not have a back-up aquarium, or you may need to quarantine a specific frog, a temporary living set-up is must. However, you need to remember that this living set-up is only temporary until you have finished the quarantine or you have given a larger and more suitable home for your frog.

Setting Up a Temporary Terrarium

1. You need to have a jar with a lid. Rinse it thoroughly, dry both the jar and the lid, and screw the lid on the jar.

2. Pound holes on the jar's lid, this will be used for air, you can use a hammer and a nail. Have six to eight nails, so the airway would be enough. Remove the lid from the jar.

3. Place the jar sideways, on the floor. Put gravel on the bottom of the jar.

4. Put some moss, lichens, and fern over the gravel.

5. Pour in some water and make sure that the gravel is not thoroughly soaked.

6. Put a dried twig in the jar.

7. Place your frog and put the lid back. Make sure you put the jar in a slightly lighted area.

Setting Up a Frog Terrarium:

1. Soak the substrate of your choosing in a bucket of warm water. The water to substrate ratio is 2 to 1. Let it sit for 15-20 minutes.

2. Rinse the bedding but leave out 20% moisture.

3. Spread the substrate through the terrarium floor. It should be around 1.5 to two times thicker that the frog of your choosing.

4. Make sure that there are no sharp edges of the logs and plants. Place other accessories such as logs, plants, water dishes, and etc. around the terrarium. Remember, live plants could help retain moisture as well as moss. Arrange the terrarium so your frog has a place to hunt, hide, and explore.

5. Put a thermometer and hydrometer in a place you can easily see but a place where your frog can't easily get it.

6. Use a mister or put an automatic mister to humidify your aquarium.

7. Put a heat lamp on the terrarium lid. Lids are important as your frog can climb out of the habitat. Other than that, make sure you put the heat lamp is inaccessible for your pet. If your frog could touch this, this would burn the frog.

Filtration and Cleaning

You may need to clean the aquarium just the same way as you do it for most freshwater fish. However, you need to do it routinely as your frog will shed more often.

If you plan to have a half and half set-up, figure out how to get a filter that would work, but not affect the land substrate. You can have under gravel filter, just the same as the over-the side filters.

Cleaning your Frog Aquarium

Although frogs are pretty low-maintenance pets, you still need to provide them with clean environment to keep them healthy. These little creatures shed regularly, secrete mucus through their skin, bathe in their water bowls, eat live animals, which would contribute greatly on the waste built-up in their tank.

You need to clean the entire frog aquarium regularly, as well as to change the water to prevent both bacterial and fungal infection. It would be tiresome experience at first, but it would not really take much time soon enough. What you will need to clean your frog terrarium:

- chlorine treatment tablets
- paper towels
- colander
- scrub brush
- temporary housing / jar

Here are the steps in cleaning your frog's aquarium:

Step #1: Prepare the water ahead. Make sure you already have chlorine - free water that you would use on your tank. You need to leave the water sitting overnight.

Step #2: Remove the frog and place them in a temporary place, just like in a jar, if you plan to do a complete and thorough cleaning. If you do not want to prepare a jar, you can buy a small plastic tank with the sole purpose for cleaning. These tanks are easily available in most pet stores. However, if you are just tidying up and changing the water, you can leave the frog sitting in the frog.

Step #3: Remove 25% to 75% of water from your African Bullfrog's tank. The percentage of water would easily depend on how dirty the water is and how long you have made a partial water change. You may use a siphon hose, filter, or a plastic container to remove the water.

Step #4: Remove most of the substrate or gravel from the bottom of your tank, especially if you are doing a thorough cleaning and sanitizing to treat some common disease. If you are just spot cleaning, it is key to leave some substrate and gravel behind. Put your substrate on a fine colander, then use a hot water and scrub brush to clean away the debris or any algae present. Rinse well and have it air dry for some time.

Step #5: Inspect if there are any pieces of food hidden inside your frog's aquarium or any uneaten insects on it. Remove anything that you can find. If you leave things on the tank, this would promote bacteria and fungi growth that would seriously affect your pet's health. Also see the skin shedding of your pet, you can inspect it and see if your frog is healthy.

Step #6: Remove all the plastic plants and decorative items. Make sure you scrub them thoroughly and rinse well and return these things to the tank.

Step #7: Wipe the outside and inside of the aquarium with toilet papers. Remember; do not clean the tank walls with any chemical cleaners as they are very harmful to your pets.

Step #8: Replace the substrate or gravel carefully and slowly.

Step #9: Put new water to the frog aquarium to carefully replace the water you have removed. If your frogs are purely aquatic, refill the tank. If they are just terrestrial, replace the water from the frog's swimming area.

Step #10: Return your frog. Give them enough time to adjust to the new and clean environment before you disturb them again.

Waster Removal

Waste removal is a frequent upkeep that you need to do in your terrarium.

Uneaten and left over insects could seriously create a lot of wastes. These dead insects would create molds and would become a source of unwanted waste. Remove these things as soon as possible.

Rotting and fallen plants are another form of waste that is often overlooked. If you see a plant that is starting to rot or die, you need to have it removed immediately. A large dying plant in your African Bullfrog's tank could create too much waste that the aquarium could handle. However, fallen leaves that are left to decompose on their own usually do not present a grave problem. Other common wastes include skin shedding, infertile eggs, animal feces.

A terrarium that you have set-up for a few months, it should have a lot of beneficial bacteria that would help take care of the waste. In addition, there are a lot of microorganism and small helpful invertebrates you can introduce in a terrarium. You can do this by mixing leaf compost from outside into the substrate or soil.

Husbandry - related concerns and housing problems

In some cases, you may come across problems concerning the husbandry that you have set-up for your pet. You might have overlooked some things because it might look teeny tiny to you.

Water quality

Your frog is relying on water for its life. A small alteration in the water quality could lead up to significant diseases, and could sometimes, lead to death.

If you believe your frog is sick and planning to take it to the vet, make sure to bring a sample of the water as well. However, do not bring your pet in the water, instead, put the water in another container and bring it to you for the frog's exam, so the water could be tested for quality issues.

Your vet will evaluate dissolved oxygen, pH, chlorine, pathogens (bacteria), nitrate or nitrite, ammonia, and harness. In these parameters, if some of it out of range, it will be easily corrected.

Problems concerning chlorine and ammonia could be easily treated with sodium thiosulfate baths or fresh water baths. The nitrite and nitrate issues may respond to methylene blue baths.

Dehydration for Amphibians

Many amphibians need an aquatic environment. Aside from that, the need a specific humidity in the enclosure or they might suffer chronic dehydration or even worse, desiccation.

Some amphibians can handle a certain degree of dehydration, in some cases; some can even handle 30% without suffering from extreme damages.

Unfortunately, some animals do not respond positively to dehydration, some may even succumb to kidney damages after a few days to a few weeks.

Some symptoms of dehydration are sunken eyes in their sockets, dry to tacky skin, color changes, and a thick slim coat. Your African Bullfrog will have a decreased activity as well as its food intake.

You can easily correct this problem by placing the amphibian in chlorine - free, well - oxygenated water at its preferred and well-maintained body temperature.

In rare cases, you may need to give them supplemental fluid. Immediately bring your frog to your vet to administer replacement fluid intracoelomically in certain situations.

Trauma for Amphibians

Most of amphibian's skin is delicate. A slight human touch could cause their skin extreme damage. Transport bags or even abrasive nets could harm the slime layer and the skin. If you need to handle your African Bullfrog, you need to wear wet latex gloves that are cleaned thoroughly with chlorine free water before you touch African Bullfrog.

Cage furniture, plants, rocks, and substrate could cause abrasion to their rostrum, feet, skin, and belly. Once the skin is damaged, the risk for infection increases dramatically.

Bite wounds, rubbing nose on the glass or skins, fighting, and any other physical barrier could be a source of potential infection. You need to cover your glass covering with paint, change your metal screen to soft nylon, and separate animals from sizes, especially the aggressive ones.

You need to ask your vet how to give first aid on these injuries or even systemic antibiotics and pain medications as your frog needs it.

Amphibian Hypothermia and Hyperthermia

Hypothermia is not really that life threatening if you caught this early. The frog could be slowly rewarmed to its proper temperature. If you have exposed it to cool temperatures for long periods of time, immunosuppression is possible, as well as deleterious effects on the African Bullfrog's gastrointestinal tract.

If your Pixie frog has recently eaten and then exposed to extreme temperature that would be too cool for digestion, intestinal upset and vomiting could result.

Aside from this, hyperthermia is not really lethal if you catch it early. Some signs of hyperthermia include uncoordinated limbs, hyperactivity, lethargy, and ultimately, death. Just like hypothermia, your African Bullfrog should be placed in fresh, chlorine-free water at its proper temperature to increase the body temperature.

If your animal have been severely heat stressed, it may need vet intervention to have fluids and corticosteriods injected.

Amphibian Toxicities

Your African Bullfrog is extremely sensitive to its environmental toxins, due to their permeable skin and their high surface area to body weight ration.

Iodine, quanternary ammonium, ammonia, chlorihexidine, and chlorine are some disinfectants that are highly toxic to your amphibian. Many of these things could be easily absorbed in plastic containers and would possibly leech out. So even though you do not see the disinfectant, you need to use a glass or stainless steel for your pet African Bullfrog.

Reddening of skin, increase mucus production in its skin, blood spots on the skin, difficulty in breathing, hyperactivity to lethargy, convulsions, tremors, paralysis, vomiting, diarrhea, and death are some signs of toxicity. However, the toxins and its signs vary greatly in species.

Cigarette smoke and pesticides are shown to be toxic to amphibians. You need to keep your pet in a smoke free environment.

Things to Remember:

- You need to mist your terrarium around two to three times a day to prevent the substrate from rotting.

- You need to have a lamp on during the day to evaporate the excess moisture content in your terrarium. Excess moisture could cause mold to grow.

- Make sure to use deodorizer and disinfectant to remove the mold inside the terrarium.

These are the essential things that you need to purchase and do to have a conducive and healthy environment for your African Bullfrog. Keep in mind to purchase these things before you bring your frog at home. If you will not provide these things, you may compromise your frog's environment and its health

Chapter Seven: Health Considerations

When you get an African Bullfrog, you are committing to a lifelong relationship that would start from the first moment you purchase it and until its death.

You need to commit in giving the best for your pet, you will start with giving a conducive and healthy environment that could mimic its real habitat. An aquarium would be a great place for you to place your pet in. Aside from this, you also need to give the best food possible for your pet to have complete nutritional benefits. You also need to supplement the food with vitamin A and D.

However, there are times that your pet African Bullfrog will get sick. Although your pet will rarely get sick, there will be times that you need to face the music. This portion will give you an insight of the possible diseases that your pet would have in the near future. Keep an open eye as these things might happen to your African Bullfrog soon.

The Tell - Tale Signs

Most frogs tend to be generally healthy and long-lived. However, there might be tell-tale signs. You need to evaluate the living conditions such as wrong temperature, high levels of ammonia, finding traces of water, fouled soil, and excessive light. This could contribute to depressed immune system and illness. Here are some tell-tale signs to know whether or not your frog is sick:

1. Your frog might have unusual behavior.
2. There is a gradual or sudden weight loss. You can see weight loss around the abdominal area, which starts

to look hollow, and you may even see the outline the backbones and hipbones.

3. There is an excessive digestive gas that is associated with overeating, intestinal parasites, oversized prey, intestinal infection, gas bubble disease, or even respiratory infection.

4. There might be red blotches that are caused by hemorrhaging, or white blotched that is caused by fungi.

5. You can see that there is a fuzziness or cloudiness in the frog's eyes.

6. There is a general swelling in the frog's head, body, or even the limb. This could be the result of poor water quality to bacterial infection, kidney diseases that would cause edema.

7. Your pet could spend too much time in hiding.

8. It is drinking or eating less, and there is a tremendous weight loss. However, before you judge that your frog is not eating, you need to give a variety of food before you judge that it is sick. If you think that it is

truly sick, bring a stool sample to your vet. If it does not have any stool, you need to bring in a whole frog.

9. You can see discolored skin.

10. The joints are swollen.

11. There is a great discharge from the nose, eyes, or mouth.

12. You can see runny droppings that would occur for more than two days.

13. The frog is spending too much time in the water. Excessive bathing is actually unusual.

14. If you see that frogs are yawning too much, this could be a symptom of a disease with no cure.

You can prevent this and give your pet a good health and long life through designing and maintaining a terrarium, you should also manage its temperature, water quality, light, furnishing, topography, and diet needs of your frog. You need to constantly check these conditions because this plays a critical role in preventing the onset of diseases.

Ways to Keep Your Pixie Frog Healthy

These are some ways to keep your African Bullfrog healthy:

- Give a Vitamin D in the diet.

- Do not handle new pixie frogs in its first few days with you; have them get settled in your new environment.

Common Health Concerns

There are a lot of diseases that are great health concerns for you as a pet owner. This disease might occur or could possibly happen in the future.

Frog Chytrid Fungus

This occurs for lowland and upland stream frogs. This disease was discovered in 1999 but could be responsible for the decline of the frog population in the 1970.

There are spores of fungus that grows of the outer layers of the frog's skin; this would then result to keratin damage that would kill your frog in 10 to 18 days.

The spores of this fungus can be transported via wet soil or water.

Metabolic Bone Disease

This is a common disease among the captive amphibian, such as the African Bullfrog. This would cause deformities and soft bones in the skeletal system.

If you are not giving your frog food that is enriched with calcium or calcium + D3, your frog would develop metabolic bone disease.

The signs of this disease are failure to grab prey, droopy lower jaw, muscle twitching, backbone and pelvic deformities, and listlessness.

You can treat this disease through consistently coating the food with calcium and vitamin D. However, if your frog is having a hard time grabbing the prey, because the bones are too soft, you would need to administer the calcium + D3 with a syringe through the frog's mouth once every one to two days until the frog's bones start to harden.

Toxic - Out Syndrome

You need to ensure that your frog's water is changed frequently because your pet African Bullfrog absorbs water through their skin. If you ever leave foul water in the substrate, some toxins could be absorbed through your pet's skin – which will eventually lead to a disorder.

Spastic extension of hind limbs, cloudy eyes, erratic jumping, and listlessness are some of the symptoms of the toxic out syndrome.

You can easily treat this disease by placing your frog in a shallow water dish of clean water then you leave your frog there.

You need to replace the water every four hours or until the signs of the syndrome goes away.

You need to closely monitor the outside conditions so you can protect your from having this toxic out syndrome.

Water Edema Syndrome

In this syndrome, your frog will start to swell up because of too much water retention. In very rare cases, your African Bullfrog may feel like a water bag.

Some common causes of this disease are a damaged lymph heart and kidney disease. Unfortunately, there is no known information as to how to prevent this disorder.

You may limit the amount of water available to the frog, or your trusty vet could release retained water through small incisions at specific swell sites, but this will be a very tedious process.

Bacterial Infection

Your beloved frog is regularly exposed to bacteria, but sometimes, the bacteria are fought off by their mighty immune system.

If your African Bullfrog is stressed out paired with an depressed immune system, the bacteria can fully invade.

Some stressful conditions are foul water, overcrowding, and improper temperature. You need o make sure that you can provide proper husbandry to lessen the risk of your frog's stress.

Loss of appetite, listlessness, redness on the underside of the thighs and belly, excessive skin slough, skin shedding, loss of appetite are some signs of bacterial infection.

If you do not notice this infection, there could be more extreme neurological signs. Bring your frog to the vet immediately; s/he will prescribe tretracycline bath and antibiotics. These baths may become stressful and could be very ineffective.

Fungal Infection

The fungal infection could infect scrapes or wounds, which is very common for tadpoles. This infection could be easily treated topically by removing your African Bullfrog from the water and daubing mercurochrom, malachite green, or hydrogen peroxide.

Amphibian Hypovitaminosis A

This is a common result of low vitamin A in the frog diet, or also known as the short tongue syndrome.

Squamos Metaplasia is a condition that is a result of low vitamin A level. Your African Bullfrog will have an inability to produce proper sticky mucus that is needed on its tongue.

You can easily see this when your toad or frog tries to grasp the prey properly, and it does not stick easily to the tongue when it is retracted into its mouth, and its prey easily goes away.

Aside from the aforementioned signs, hypovitaminosis A could easily affect the cnjuctiva around the frog's eyes (just like swelling) as well as the kidney and bladder infection that would lead to hydrocoelom.

The treatment of this disease will involve life threatening conditions and supplementing vitamin A in the diet, as well as correcting the frog's diet and any other underlying cause.

Endoparasites

Tapeworms, roundworms, and pinworms are very common among toads and frogs. Some of these endoparasites are not really that harmful for your frog, but if you see a parasite, immediately consult your vet. S/he will diagnose the parasites and treat it before it gets too late.

Parasites are easily transferable, so make sure you quarantine new amphibians before you introduce new pets to your old pets.

Amphibian Corneal Lipidosis

Some characteristics of this disease include whitish plaques, deposition of cholesterol deposit in the cornea.

The cause of this disease includes high cholesterol level which is result of diet high in fat. There is no strict treatment for this, but you may correct the diet to prevent the condition to further worsen.

Gout

This condition is the deposition of uric acid crystal in different location in your African Bullfrog's body. The cause of this problem includes diet that is very high in purine, infection, dehydration, and kidney failure.

The crystal will slowly form in soft tissues such as the kidney and liver, but could form larger stones that you can find in the bladder. If your vet already diagnosed this, it is actually sever now. These bladder stones can be easily removed by your vet.

Amphibian Viruses

Your African Bullfrog is very susceptible to various viral diseases. The most common virus that your African

Bullfrog easily contract is the herpes virus. The herpes virus causes kidney tumors. This would affect the kidney, which will cause hydrops and hydrocoelom.

Your animal would easily lose weight and would die after spawning. Another virus is the Iridoviruses, specifically the ranaviruses, is the subject form many years. These viruses are responsible for eradication certain breeds of frogs.

Generally, amphibian viruses are very uncommon to general population. However, more of them is slowly being discovered because of the increased interest in the disease in both wild and captive specimen.

Fungal Infection

One of the most common fungi among the amphibians is the Batrachochytrium Dendrobatidis, which is the agent of chytridiomycosis. Although most of the fungal infections are seen in immunocompromised amphibians, B. dendrobatidis could cause disease in healthy frogs.

Signs of this B. dendrobatidis could vary from sudden death to no sign to slowly onset, starting with the reddening of the belly (which is similary for dermatosepticemia), excessive skin shedding, and lethargy. If you catch this early, treatment could be very effective.

There are also other fungal organisms that could cause disease in amphibians. Saprolegniasis would produce cotton-like growth on the mouth and skin of your African Bullfrog.

Chromomycosis, a pigmented fungus, could be seen in various amphibians. It would produce light-tan to dark-gray nodules on the African Bullfrog's skin. If you do not treat this, this would result to death.

Most of these fungal diseases are the result of underlying poor environmental condition and stress. You need to correct these deficiencies because this is mandatory to have a successful treatment and prevention for other future diseases.

Amphibian Parasites

Amphibians are also prone to various parasites. This includes protozoa, trematodes, nematodes, and cestodes.

Entamoeba ranarum and Amoebiasis are very common and can be treated easily if you catch this early. Roundworms, also called the nematodes, are the most common parasites seen in amphibians.

Lungworm, also known the rhabdias, could be easily found in small numbers. This is contagious to other amphibians, so, if you have an affected animal, you must quarantine it and keep it separated until you have properly treated it.

Neoplasia

Cancer and tumors, also called the neoplasia, is very common to your African Bullfrog. Some common form of cancers is of the kidney, gonads, liver, and skin. Some symptoms will include hydrocoelom.

Blindness

Your African Bullfrog's blindness is primarily caused by lipids on the corneas. Aside from this, there is also a high fat diet because you may have fed too much pinkie mice in its diet.

At this moment, there is no cure for this disease, but you can prevent this disorder by feeding your frog a low-fat diet.

Impaction

Impaction depends where you house your frog. Your frog could ingest some of substrate when they are trying to grab a prey. Some small gravel could be easily passed through the feces, but larger gravel could remain in the intestinal tract that could cause the blockage.

To prevent this impaction, you can provide alternate substrate to your African bullfrog. If you see that your frog is impacted, you may feel your frog's belly, and if there is a hard lump, there is probably a substrate that your frog could not digest.

In rare cases, your frog might excrete the substrate slowly throughout a period of weeks. If the condition continues to persist, consult the vet immediately to have it removed.

Obesity

Your frog will reach a larger size when it becomes an adult, so you just need to balance it out with a little food to maintain a healthy weight.

Most people would increase food intake for the adult frogs in order to increase the frog's size. Some may even size up their preys. But a bigger prey would be very dangerous for the frog's health. Here is a recommended feeding schedule for your frog:

- Supplement a 3 week old cricket every one to two days for froglets up to two inches

- Froglets from two to four inches could be fed with three week old crickets, mice that has been killed that is dipped in calcium, or even supplemented worms ever two or three days.

- When you frog becomes an adult, growing into four to five inches, you need to supplement the worms or crickets or nightcrawlers, mice every seven to 10 days.

These are just some of the things that you need to do concerning your pet's health. Make sure to thoroughly check your pet's substrate and look for signs of foul health. Make sure you also continue to feed the right amount with the frequency at the right time. Not feeding your pet correctly could cause you problems in the near future.

Keep in Mind!

We have tackled a lot about the African Bullfrog. We hope you have decided to try to take care of this exotic breed. You need to be committed to taking care of this pet; they will live as long 20 years! You need to provide its housing, feeding, and even during its sick days. You need to give a sustainable house for the pet as to make it comfy and give it a happy and healthy home. Providing a healthy home is not an easy task, you need to give a great aquarium that your pet would truly enjoy. Aside from this, you need to have the feeding considerations as your pet has a strict feeding guide. If you think you can handle this, you can purchase your very first pet!

Remember to check your frog's environment regularly as this greatly affects your African Bullfrog. These are the essential things you need to know about the African Bullfrog. Make sure you bookmark this page and highlight all these things because they are all equally important. Remember these things because these are the most important stuff in this book. Go out now and get your very first African Bullfrog!

Glossary of Frog Terms

Advertisement Call - Males frogs 'and toads ' mating call

Aggressive Call- Territorial Call; it is a call made by male when another male comes too close

Amphibian- double life; animals that are vertebrates and lives a part of their lives in water

Amplexus- A position wherein the male frog is on the top of a female in order to externally fertilize the eggs

Anura- tail-less; the order of toads and frogs

Archaeobatrachia- ancient frogs

Army- a collective term used to define a group of frogs

Aquatic- lives in water

Bask- to sit under the sunlight in order to warm up

Beaufort Wind Scale- a kind of scale used to monitor and estimate the speed of the wind

Binomial Nomenclature- biological name assigned to every living thing

Boss- an area on the toad's head between the eyes that is raised

Carnivore- species that eat meat

Chorus- a large group of singing, calling toads and/or frogs

Chytridiomycosis (BD) - Chytrid; a fungus of frogs that affects their skin's permeability

CITES - The Convention on International Train Endangered Species of wild fauna and flora

Citizen Scientists- citizens who contribute scientific information for various researches and projects worldwide

Cold-blooded- Ectothermic

Detritus- decaying animal matter and plant settling at the bottom of the pond

Digits- toes or fingers

Distress call- a call made by a frog or toad in order to discourage a predator

Dorsal- upper side

Dorsolateral- stripes or parallel folds along the back of a frog

Ecosystem- the interaction between the environment and living organisms

Ectothermic- the ability of a specie to control its body temperature through the use of available surroundings

Genera- related species that share the same first name

Habitat- it is where plant, animals, and other species live and grow

Herbivore- a specie that feeds on plant

Herpetologist- a scientist who studies amphibians and reptiles

Herpetology- The study of Amphibians and Reptiles

Insectivore- a specie that feeds on insect

Invasive Species- species that are not native to an area and cause ecological harm

Invertebrate- a specie without a backbone

Knot- a group of toads

Lateral- side surface

Mesobatrachia- Middle Frogs

Metamorphosis- stages of change that a specie undergo

Nictating Membrane- inner eyelid which is transparent

Paratoid glands- toxin glands found behind the eyes of toads

Phenology- Study of the Seasonal Timing of Events

Polyplois- having one or more than one sets of chromosomes

Pollywog- tadpole

Pupil- part of the eye on which the light enters

Ranavirus- a kind of disease of amphibians

Release call- a call made by a female when she's not yet ready or a call made by a male if another male thought he's a female

Spawn- eggs of frogs and toads

Submerged- beneath the surface

Tadpole- a frog's larval stage

Taxonomy- classifying all living things based on their similarities and differences

Territorial Call- Aggressive Call

Tibial gland- a gland found on the lower leg

Toe Pads- sticky area on the toes

Tubercle- Rough area on a toad's body

Tympanum- eardrum

Ventral- refers to the lower surface of the body or belly

Vernal Pools- Temporary ponds that are filled with water seasonally as the snow melts or when it rains

Vocal sac- an expandable sac found beneath the frog/toad's throat

Wetland- wet area between deep water and uplands

Index

D

E

F

G

H

I

Photo Credits

Page Photo by user Steven & Courtney Johnson via Flickr.com,

https://www.flickr.com/photos/unnormalized/2769739876/

Page Photo by user mrpolyonymous via Flickr.com,

https://www.flickr.com/photos/mrpolyonymous/10053182263/

Page Photo by user C_Phif via Flickr.com,

https://www.flickr.com/photos/60097993@N02/35779648426/

Page Photo by user something.from.nancy via Flickr.com,

https://www.flickr.com/photos/carradine65/115563057/

Page Photo by user Josh More via Flickr.com,

https://www.flickr.com/photos/guppiecat/365436309/

Page Photo by user Bernard DUPONT via Flickr.com,

https://www.flickr.com/photos/berniedup/12618902215/

Page Photo by user David Ellis via Flickr.com,

https://www.flickr.com/photos/david44149/32635360376/

Page Photo by user Bernard DUPONT via Flickr.com,

https://www.flickr.com/photos/berniedup/6045769166/

References

"These classic-looking frogs are not cuddly pets" – The Spruce Pets

https://www.thesprucepets.com/african-bullfrogs-1238715

"Frog Care 101: What You Need to Know Before You Get a Frog" – PetMD.com

https://www.petmd.com/reptile/care/evr_rp_frog-care-101-what-you-need-know-you-get-frog#

"African Bullfrog" - OregonZoo.org

https://www.oregonzoo.org/discover/animals/african-bullfrog-0

"African Bullfrog" - PhiladelphiaZoo.org

https://philadelphiazoo.org/Animals/Amphibians/Frogs-Toads/African-Bullfrog.aspx

"Choosing an African Giant Bullfrog" – PetPlace.com

https://www.petplace.com/article/reptiles/general/choosing-an-african-giant-bullfrog/

"African Bullfrog" – WhoZoo.org

https://whozoo.org/Intro98/markdiss/mardis.htm

"The Big and the Bold: The African Bullfrog" – AnimalScene.ph

https://animalscene.ph/2018/02/13/the-big-and-the-bold-the-african-bullfrog-pyxicephalus-adspersus/

"African Bull Frog Care Sheet" – TheAmphibian.co.uk

http://www.theamphibian.co.uk/african_bull_frog_pyxie_frog_care_sheet_pyxicephalus_adspersus.htm

"Beginner's Guide to Keeping Frogs as Pets" – Frogpets.com

http://www.frogpets.com/beginners-guide-to-keeping-frogs-as-pets/#The_Pros_Cons

"Frog Care Guide" – VetBabble.com

https://www.vetbabble.com/small-pets/frog-care-guide/

"Housing Your Pet Frog" – AllAboutFrogs.org

http://allaboutfrogs.org/info/housing/

"Substrates for Amphibians & Reptiles" – AmphibianCare.com

http://amphibiancare.com/2016/11/28/substrates-part-1/

"Setting Up Your Frog's Terrarium" – Blog About Frogs

http://blogaboutfrogs.blogspot.com/2011/01/setting-up-your-frogs-terrarium.html

"What to Feed Your Frog" – PetMD.com

https://www.petmd.com/reptile/nutrition/what-feed-your-frog

"What Do Frogs Eat" – Frogs.cc

http://frogs.cc/frogs-eat/

"What Type of Insect Should a Frog Eat" – Mom.me

https://animals.mom.me/type-insect-should-frog-eat-5729.html

"Frog Diets – Nutritious Foods for Popularly – Kept Frogs and Toads" – ThatPetPlace.com

http://blogs.thatpetplace.com/thatreptileblog/2010/10/07/frog-diets-nutritious-foods-for-popularly-kept-frogs-and-toads/

"African Bullfrog Care, Feeding and Terrarium Design" – ThatPetPlace.com

http://blogs.thatpetplace.com/thatreptileblog/2013/11/22/african-bullfrog-care-feeding-terrarium-design/

"Life Cycle of a Frog" – AllAboutFrogs.org

http://allaboutfrogs.org/weird/general/cycle.html

"Frog Reproduction, from Mating to Metamorphosis" – HowStuffWorks.com

https://animals.howstuffworks.com/amphibians/frog4.htm

"Building a Rainchamber to Breed Your Frogs" – PollyWogsWorldOfFrogs.com

http://www.pollywogsworldoffrogs.com/Text-html/rainchamber.html

"Breeding Your Frogs" – PollyWogsWorldOfFrogs.com

http://www.pollywogsworldoffrogs.com/Text-html/frog-breeding.html

"Caring for Tadpoles—From Egg to Froglet" – PetHelpful.com

https://pethelpful.com/reptiles-amphibians/How-And-What-To-Feed-Tadpoles

"Sick Frogs and Salamanders" – ReptilesMagazine.com

http://www.reptilesmagazine.com/Frogs-Amphibians/Sick-Frogs-And-Amphibians/

"Becoming Frogs: How to Collect, House, and Feed Healthy Tadpoles" – The Spruce Pets

https://www.thesprucepets.com/raising-tadpoles-1238727

"A Set – up Guide for Your New Pixie Frog" – PetSmart.com

https://www.petsmart.com/learning-center/reptile-care/a-set-up-guide-for-your-new-pixie-frog/A0183.html#help_healthy

"If you think your frog or toad is sick" – Frogdaze.com

http://www.frogdaze.com/the-frog-doctor.html

"Frog Diseases" – WetTropics.gov.au

http://www.wettropics.gov.au/frog-diseases

"Common Illness in Pac Man Frogs" – PetHelpful.com

https://pethelpful.com/reptiles-amphibians/pac-man-frog-health

CPSIA information can be obtained
at www.ICGtesting.com
Printed in the USA
BVHW051036090622
639231BV00009B/912